DATE DUE			

BLACK HILLS, WHITE SKY

BLACK HILLS, WHITE SKY

Photographs from the Collection of the
Arvada Center Foundation, Inc.

Selected and with Commentary by
ALVIN M. JOSEPHY, JR.

NYT
Times
BOOKS

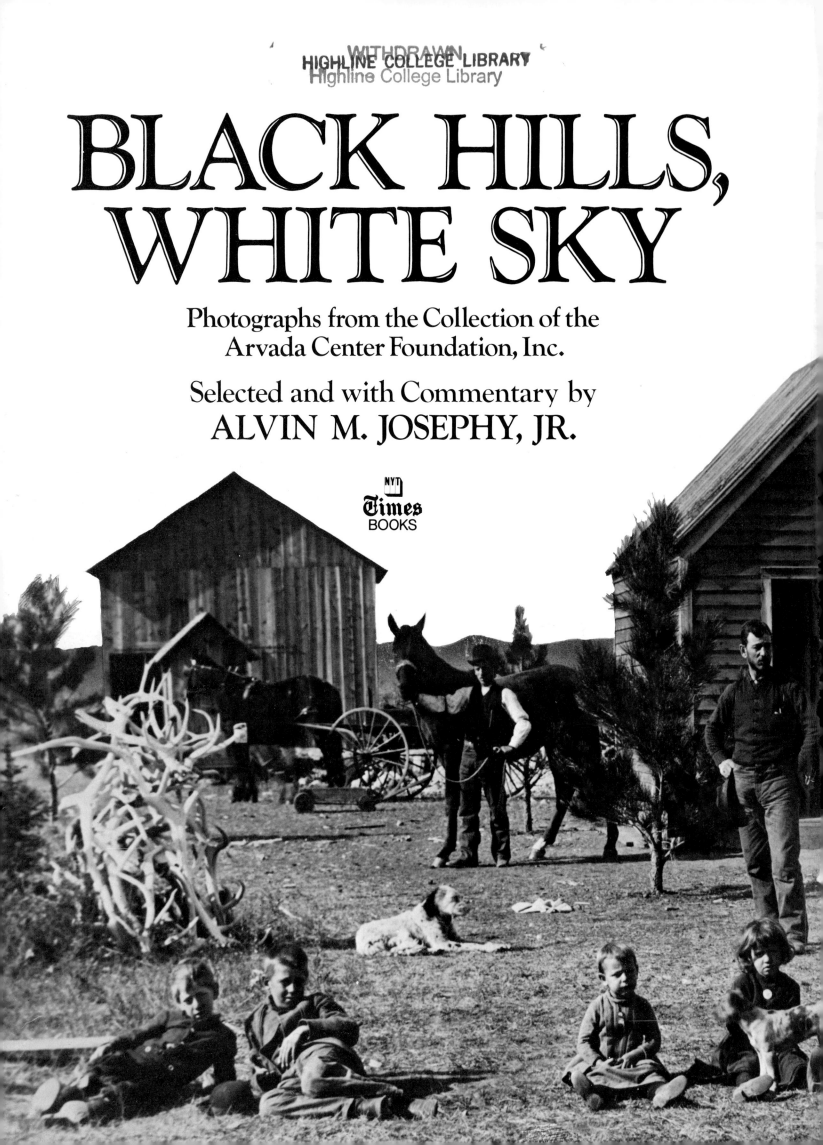

Published by TIMES BOOKS, a division
of Quadrangle/The New York Times Book Co., Inc.
Three Park Avenue, New York, N.Y. 10016

Published simultaneously in Canada by
Fitzhenry & Whiteside, Ltd., Toronto

Library of Congress Cataloging in Publication Data
Josephy, Alvin M., 1915-
    Black Hills, white sky.

    Photos by W. J. Collins and others.
    1. Black Hills, S. D. and Wyo.—History—
Pictorial works. 2. Frontier and pioneer
life—Black Hills—Pictorial works. I. Collins,
William J., 1867-1938. II. Title.
F657.B6J73 978.3'9 78-58173
ISBN 0-8129-0789-2

Manufactured in the United States of America

DESIGNED BY BETH TONDREAU
WITH ASSISTANCE FROM JOY TAYLOR

Contents

Introduction
by ALVIN M. JOSEPHY, Jr.

THE REMARKABLE PHOTOGRAPHS in this book, most of them previously unknown, are of a special place and time in America's past—precisely, the famed Black Hills of South Dakota between approximately 1886 and 1915. At first glance, one may wonder at their significance, for they were taken in a part of the country rich in dramatic storybook history —where, for instance, the flamboyant General Custer boasted that his Seventh Cavalry could whip all the Indians in the Northwest, and then set in motion the events that ended with his death at the Little Bighorn; where Calamity Jane, dressed in men's clothes and "built like a busted bale of hay," got her name, allegedly for the venereal disease she spread among gold miners; and where Wild Bill Hickok was shot dead in the back at a poker table while holding black aces and eights and the Jack of Diamonds, known forever after as the "deadman's hand." The Black Hills are filled with such lore, but these pictures—the work of a man named William J. Collins and several other local and itinerant frontier photographers, about whom more will shortly be said—show something different. Serene and unmelodramatic, they are, by and large, images of an everyday life, of the normal routines of unsung people who were not important enough to be immortalized in history books or legends.

And yet the photographs throb with a history of a most stirring and convincing kind, for they constitute a living, thirty-year record of ordinary but very real people of yesterday, who were engaged in the determined act of taming a raw western frontier and turning it into a part of our modern American nation. Here are views of rugged nineteenth-century mining and lumber camps and the pioneer men and women who built and graced them in the virgin forests and mountains, hard on the heels of the recently dispossessed Sioux Indians of Sitting Bull and Crazy Horse. They are pictures of road crews, railroad builders, and guardian soldiers; of emigrant settlers and their rough log homesteads; of cattle men and the longhorn herds they drove up from Texas; of farm families and townspeople; and of the trim frame homes, livery stables, schools, churches, hotels, and business establishments they reared to create a vigorous civilization in this western land.

It is wondrous that photographs like these are so vivid and real that they magically bridge the gap of generations and make the subjects seem still alive and breathing after almost a century. In addition, they are rich with the details of those bygone days and of the people they portray. Look closely at the pictures of the Scandinavian emigrants dressed in the finery they brought with them to the Black Hills from the old country, in the 1880's. Or look at the non-Hollywood work clothes of the cowboys, the miners, and the sawmill workers, and at the scenes of daily struggle and loneliness, of group activities, outings, and community affairs. These images, indeed, are basic American history, not only significant as a reliable source of myriad pieces of information that add life and substance to written history, but as an intimate illumination of a part of the heritage bequeathed to us by our ancestors. The everyday activities of people and communities revealed in the photographs are particularly meaningful to historians because they portray what time has obscured and provide visual answers to what might previously have been uncertain or unknown. But to all of us they make entirely clear and plausible what we often overlook, and what helps us appreciate history more as an aid in our own lives and affairs—that the past was lived and coped with by people just like ourselves.

The setting of the photographs—the Black Hills—is a forested mountain oasis rising more than 4,000 feet above the high grassland plains of southwestern South Dakota. Formed when a batholith with a granitic core thrust up from the earth's interior even before the Rocky Mountains were created farther to the west, it received its name from the Sioux, or Dakota Indians, who regarded its dense pine stands, mountainous slopes and valleys, and flowered parks and meadows as the sacred abode of the supernatural and called it, for the distant appearance of its wooded heights, *Paha Sapa,* "the hills that are black." For years it was the heartland of hunting territory claimed by the tribes of the Teton, or Western, Sioux, and was so recognized by the U.S. government in a treaty signed with the Sioux in 1868. Hardly was the ink dry, however, when white gold-seekers began to pressure the government to permit them to prospect in the Hills.

Rumors of the existence of gold in the Black Hills, supported by occasional finds by adventurous loners, who for brief periods braved the Indians' hostility, had persisted since 1803. But, until 1874, the region was "off limits" to whites, and no gold rush had developed. In that year, however, largely as a result of the increasing pressure to open the Hills to prospectors, an army expedition under General (then Lieutenant Colonel) George Armstrong Custer, accompanied by a number of civilian scientists and professional miners, explored the Black Hills, violating the 1868 treaty, according to the angry Sioux, who dubbed Custer's route "the thieves' trail." Several members of the expedition found gold, and the ensuing publicity led inevitably to a stampede, which the government, despite the efforts of troops who attempted to turn back the miners, could not halt.

For a time, the government tried to induce the Sioux to sell the Black Hills, but when that failed, federal officials in desperation ordered the Indians to leave the area and go peaceably onto reservations. Many of the Sioux refused. The army was directed to round them up, and the resulting campaign led to Custer's defeat and death at the Little Bighorn. The Indians had won a battle, but could not win the war, however, and, eventually, starvation and the ceaseless harassment by troops crushed their ability to resist. In the fall of 1876, the government finally coerced a number of disheartened chiefs into signing away the Indians' rights to the Black Hills, and when Congress ratified the treaty on February 28, 1877, the Hills were at last legally opened to white settlement.

By that time, one of the great gold rushes of the nation's history had been underway for two years. Despite the fact that the Hills were still Indian

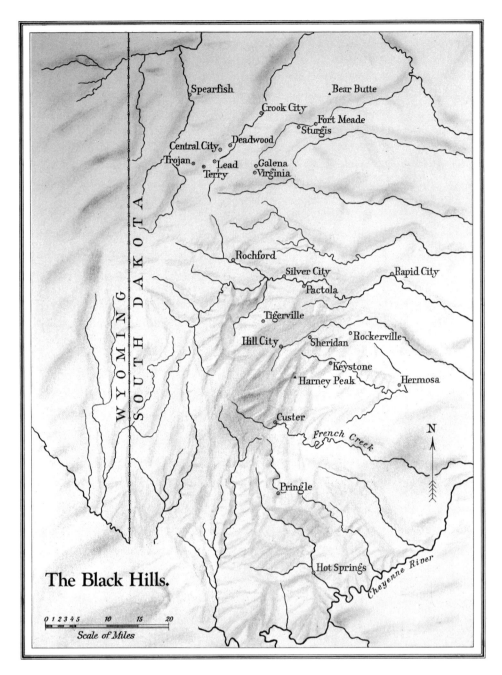

The Black Hills.

0 1 2 3 4 5   10   15   20
Scale of Miles

property, miners had poured into them in 1875 and 1876, finding gold in numerous areas and establishing booming camps that grew quickly into boisterous frontier settlements and towns. Over the winter of 1875-76, several thousand gold-seekers were in the vicinity of the new town of Custer in the central Hills, where the first diggings were located. But in March, 1876, word came of a rich strike in the northern Hills, and by mid-summer, 25,000 people were in Deadwood Gulch, among them such characters as Hickok and Calamity Jane. In a matter of months, the Hills were dotted with centers of population—Deadwood, Lead, Pactola, Hill City, Keystone, Central City, Custer, and others—inhabited by miners, merchants, gamblers, women camp followers, and others who had gone from one rush to another in the West.

Inevitably, the easy pickings on the surface played out, and deep, hard-rock mining, requiring the investment of capital, replaced placer mining. Individuals who had panned for themselves at streams or worked in cooperative groups with rockers and sluice boxes went to work for syndicates and corporations that dug into the mountains. They took out gold in horse-drawn carts, and erected hoisting sheds and costly stamp mills. But others abandoned mining and found jobs in the new settlements or turned to farming. Their ranks were gradually increased by newcomers—emigrant groups from Europe, farm families in covered wagons from east of the Missouri River, and all sorts of entrepreneurs—lured by the hope of a new start in a new land, the same hope that had characterized every western frontier.

At first, the homesteaders and new arrivals built simple buildings of logs hewn square, notched at the ends, and chinked with clay or strips of root-matted sod (on the treeless plains along the eastern fringe of the Hills, many of the earliest homes were built entirely of chunks of sod, their owners becoming known as "soddies"). Fireplaces were constructed of stones held together with mud or cement. Commercial buildings were sometimes of logs, but came to rely more on planks and "store" lumber and generally sported high false fronts rising above the ridge of the structure to give the effect of an extra story. In time, as individuals and families began to do better financially, such architecture was succeeded by squarely built, four-room frame houses, painted white, and embellished, as income grew, with second stories; wide, scrollwork-adorned porches providing shade from the summer sun; coal sheds in the rear; and cupolas frequently housing lanterns to guide home persons lost in a winter blizzard. Brickyards were at length established, and, as the towns developed, bricks, as well as quarried sandstone and granite, were used for many of the public and commercial buildings.

The tough prairie soil, the semi-arid climate, and the extremes of nature that included blinding snowstorms in winter, searing heat in summer, and fierce winds in every season made farming a trial. Moreover, the country between the Black Hills and the Missouri River was still owned by the Indians, and no rail line could be extended across it to carry the farmers' produce to the cities in the East. Until 1886, when the first rail spur was built northward to Rapid City from Nebraska, commerce to and from the Hills was conducted exclusively by stagecoaches and freight wagons drawn by oxen, horses, or mules. The principal routes ran to Deadwood, Rapid City, and Sturgis (a freighting center for the northern Hills) from Bismarck and Fort Pierre on the Missouri River and Sidney, Nebraska, and Cheyenne, Wyoming, both Union Pacific Railroad towns farther south. Rapid City, founded by four discouraged prospectors in February, 1876, on Rapid Creek, at the eastern edge of the Black Hills, benefited greatly from its location, midway between the bustling northern and southern mining centers, and grew steadily in importance as the principal trading and business mart for the whole region.

If the area was difficult for farmers, it was a paradise for cattlemen. The lush grasslands were ready-made for herds, and Texas drovers were soon arriving with longhorns that took the place of the buffalo, now all but vanished at the hands of meat and robe hunters. Ranches, comprised of rough, unpainted, and sprawling homes, low barns, bunkhouses, and corrals, were established in draws, out of the wind, and huge outfits, employing permanent and itinerant cowboys and ranch hands, carved out domains for their herds in the foothills and the adjoining rangeland of the plains. Despite occasional disastrous winters, many stockmen became prosperous in the region during the 1880's and 1890's.

In 1889, Dakota Territory, which had been created back in 1861, was divided into two states, and both North and South Dakota were admitted to the Union. In 1891, two major railroads, the North Western and the Burlington, built branch lines northward from Nebraska through the Black Hills, and the frontier aspect of the region began to fade quickly. In the mountains and gulches by that time, mining had become an industry. At Lead, the Homestake Mining Company, owned by a group headed by George Hearst, the father of William Randolph, was fast becoming a legend as a fabulously rich gold-producing property (as of 1962 it had produced almost three-quarters of a billion dollars in bullion, and it is still producing). Other corporate properties were producing silver, mica, tin, and other minerals, as well as gold. Lumbering, inaugurated during the first days of the gold rush by enterprising individuals who made use of the bounteous stands of pine to supply wood for buildings and sluices, had also become a large-scale business, meeting the demands of the growing towns, and even exporting timber out of the region. For a long time, Lead would have the largest population in the Black Hills, but Rapid City's importance as the transportation, banking, and business center of the area, once it was established, would never be seriously challenged; it continued to grow steadily as a city of substantial commerce, varied businesses, wide thoroughfares, and fine homes. By 1886 it had a daily newspaper, *The Rapid City Daily Journal*, and the following year it became the home of the South Dakota School of Mines. Modern schools and churches were built, fraternal and social groups were organized, and leisure time was spent in the pursuit of cultural and recreational activities. As a foretaste of what was to come, outings to the cool and picturesque glades and mountain lakes and streams of the Black Hills became popular in the summer, and hotels did a thriving business at the celebrated Hot Springs resort in the southern Hills.

Since the earliest days of the gold rush, frontier photographers, trundling their equipment in wagons, had visited the Black Hills. Some of them recorded historic events, and their work—though not always accurate knowledge of who took which picture, as will be explained—has long been known. William H. Illingworth traveled to the Hills with Custer in 1874 and took some memorable photographs of that controversial expedition which precipitated the gold rush. Another visiting photographer, Stanley J. Morrow, who maintained his studio in Yankton in the southeastern corner of Dakota Territory, covered both the diggings in the Hills in the heady days of 1876 and the activities of the army in trying to round up the Sioux in the area, after Custer's defeat. Though the pictures of still others who toured the Hills after Illington and Morrow, including David F. Barry and J. C. H. Grabill, have frequently been reproduced, it has long been assumed that there were additional itinerant—and even resident—photographers in the area whose identity and work were not known. Evidence that this was correct is provided by the pictures in this book, which represent part of the collection of one such long-forgotten photographer, William J. Collins, and

William J. Collins in his later years.

which comprise not only his own work, but that of several others who are still so thoroughly unknown that little, if anything, can be said about them other than that they were there.

Collins, whose own life can still only be sketched in outline, arrived in the Black Hills in 1886 when he was nineteen years old. He had been born in Ottawa, Canada, in 1867, and after finishing his formal education had served as an apprentice in an apparently well-known photographic studio in Ottawa, owned by a man named S. Jarvis. Soon afterward, he had struck off on his own and, entering the United States, had made his way westward to the Black Hills, meeting his expenses along the way by taking portraits and other pictures and developing them in his darkroom wagon. Sometime after his arrival in Rapid City, he established his studio there, though it is possible that he had first worked for, or with, someone else.

The accepted business mores of frontier photographers like Collins have resulted in frustrating tasks for present-day researchers. It was quite usual for a photographer who bought out a predecessor or competitor to acquire that person's entire stock of pictures, including negatives and prints, and thereafter put his own name on them and sell them. Though he might not actually claim that he had taken them, mixups inevitably occurred, and numerous pictures eventually became attributed to the wrong photographer or even to several different photographers. Even today, there is confusion over who took some of the best-known and most often reproduced pictures of the early West, including some of those long believed to have been made by well-publicized photographers.

Most of the pictures in this book seem certain to have been made by Collins, who conducted his studio in Rapid City, almost without competition, for forty-seven years, and who retired in 1933, locally well-known as an able and successful photographer specializing in portraits. His collection of glass-plate negatives, however, unmistakably included the work of some others which he seems to have acquired in his early days in Rapid City. Some of them appear in these pages, not only because they add breadth and interest to the place and time that all the pictures portray, but because—save in a few instances where a darkroom wagon bearing another photographer's name is visible in the background—it cannot be asserted with accuracy which pictures Collins did *not* take.

According to the best evidence so far available, several photographers seem to have preceded Collins in Rapid City, or been contemporary with him in his early career. Of those whose work is, or may be, represented in this book, the first appears to be a man named M. A. Fuller, whose darkroom wagon can be seen in some pictures. Fuller is known to have had an assistant, however, a young man named William F. (Billy) Hall, who came from Ohio, also in 1886, and later became a builder. Hall often went out with the wagon to take pictures of outings and people's homes, and the photographs showing Fuller's wagon may actually have been taken by Hall. One picture of an outing, taken about 1888-89, has indeed been identified as Hall's work by one of the persons in the picture who, at this writing, is still living in Rapid City. Eventually, Fuller, who operated as M. A. Fuller & Co., seems to have been bought out by a partnership of two photographers named Quiggle and Johnson, who, in turn, were bought out by Collins about 1903. Still another photographer, so far identified only as a Mr. Potter, who roamed the Black Hills in a horsedrawn wagon, appears also to have had some of his pictures end up in Collins' collection.

Though many of Collins' own pictures can be identified as having been taken over the years in his studio in the Lakota Block in the center of Rapid City, he, too, traveled through the Hills with a wagon. At best, photography in the field was laborious. I am indebted to Robert A. Weinstein, author of books on western photographers and an authority on frontier photography, for the following description of what was involved:

> Having arrived . . . at the chosen location—or as near as the buggy allowed—the heavy equipment was unloaded and carried on one's back to the precise spot from which to make the picture. Imagine if it were halfway up a hill or down in the bottom of a ravine as it so frequently was! The twenty-pound camera was set

up on its heavy tripod. A large sheet of plate glass was carefully cleaned, laboriously polished and then taken by the photographer either underneath a black cloth, or into a tent or light proof area on the buggy or wagon. With the awkward piece of glass balanced on the fingers of one hand, liquid collodion and ether was poured with the other hand onto the polished surface of the glass and was encouraged to spread over the surface by tilting the heavy glass back and forth until the plate was evenly coated with the sticky (and smelly) mixture.

Still in absolute darkness, the photographer quickly plunged the coated glass into a silver nitrate bath to make the mixture light sensitive and hurriedly placed the dripping wet negative into a wooden film holder. Then it was rushed to the prefocused camera outside. Once in the camera the tripod was steadied once more, the brass lens cap, shielding lens and glass plate from the light, was removed from the lens barrel, the necessary amount of seconds required for a proper exposure was counted off slowly and silently, and the cap replaced. Chemical development of the exposed negative, an equally arduous and painstaking practice in a dark area—sometimes no more than a black cloth thrown over the photographer crouching on the ground—followed immediately. Success would permit no delay.

Photography in the studio, of course, was much easier. Like most photographers, Collins employed only a few simple backdrops, one or two of which appear in a number of his pictures. His studio had a north exposure, with large windows from floor to ceiling; save for the use of a couple of spotlights in his later days, he relied entirely on natural lighting.

There is still considerable mystery concerning Collins' disposition of his collection of almost 1,500 glass-plate negatives after his retirement. According to one story, he was going to throw them away, but offered to give them to anyone who wanted them. Someone, still unknown, took them, that version says. Another account says merely that he kept them himself, storing them in boxes in a rear shed or in his own house. It is known that before he died in Rapid City on June 10, 1938, survived by his widow, a daughter, Mrs. Beulah Crockett, and a grandson, John Crockett, presently in business in Columbia, South Carolina, he gave a large number of prints from some of the negatives to the newly built Indian Museum in Rapid City. It is also known that the fragile glass-plate negatives remained forgotten and unseen until the early 1960's when a Rapid City fireplace builder named Melvin Kambak came on them, packed tightly in boxes, in a house in which he was working. It is not known to whom the house belonged. Collins' widow had died in 1956, and neither her house nor that of her daughter, Mrs. Beulah Crockett, had a fireplace.

At any rate, when Kambak showed interest in the negatives, the owner offered to give them to him. He took them, but insisted on paying a nickel apiece for them. Soon afterward, he sold them to two Rapid City men interested in photography, Larry Carper and Jack Tscharner. At the time, the latter ran the photo department of Gamble's Store in Rapid City, and he and Kambak built a special enlarger to make prints from some of the negatives. Eventually, Tscharner opened his own Jack's Camera Shop in Rapid City and began to display some of the prints. A number of them were published in the *Rapid City Journal* and were used by Carl Leedy, a local Black Hills historian, to illustrate booklets on the lore of the region. In 1966, some were acquired as illustrations for a book, *Gold in the Black Hills*, by Watson Parker, published by the University of Oklahoma Press. By that time, the men who had made the pictures seemed to have been completely forgotten; there was no mention of them, and the photographs were simply noted as being from the "Carper-Tscharner Collection."

About 1967, a New York art dealer and appraiser named Peter Nicholson, while visiting Rapid City, came on the collection in Jack's Camera Shop and bought it. When he later moved to Denver, he took the collection with him and made some large-sized prints for an exhibition in that city. In 1970, Dayton W. Canaday, Director of the South Dakota State Historical Society in Pierre, having learned of the collection, wrote to Nicholson about the possibility of having it returned to the state. Two years later, Nicholson offered to sell it to the Historical Society for $8,000, but by the time Canaday had raised the money, Nicholson had sold it to its present owner, the Arvada Center for the Arts and Humanities in Colorado. Since then, the Center, with limited funds and personnel, has been preparing a descriptive inventory of all the glass plates and has made and assembled prints of about 350 of the pictures, the best of them being mounted for public exhibit.

And so, after more than three-quarters of a century, the work of these pioneer western photographers has at last gained recognition, and a vivid, insightful record of the Black Hills as they changed from frontier to civilization has been added to the known documentation of our past. The Hills have become one of the most popular vacation centers in the nation, drawing millions annually to scores of campgrounds and resorts, to the old gold-mining towns, and to the great stone faces of Mount Rushmore. Rapid City, Deadwood, Lead, Sturgis, and other communities pulse with tourist attractions and memories of earlier days. These photographs will undoubtedly help make those memories more real.

Many persons offered me generous assistance in preparing this book. Few are still alive who could identify the scenes or people in the various pictures, and fewer still could furnish me more than clues or hearsay about the photographers and the fate of Collins' collection after his retirement in 1933. But I especially want to thank the following, all of whom gave me valuable help: John Crockett of Columbia, South Carolina; Mrs. Melvin Kambak of Rapid City; Mrs. Clara B. Lobdell, president of the Minnilusa Historical Society of Rapid City; Mrs. Jean Diggins at the Rapid City Public Library; Sally Farrar and Harriet March of the *Rapid City Journal*; Bob Lee, editor of the Sturgis, S. D., *Black Hills Press*; Dayton W. Canaday and Mrs. Bonnie Gardner of the South Dakota State Historical Society in Pierre; Robert A. Weinstein of Los Angeles; Milton Kaplan, formerly of the Library of Congress, Washington, D.C.; Peter J. Nicholson in Denver; and Peter K. Faris and his colleagues on the staff of the Arvada Center for the Arts and Humanities in Colorado. Finally, I wish to thank, also, the accomplished designer of this book, Beth Tondreau, and my wife, Elizabeth, for their patient help.

THE MINING FRONTIER

The Mines

Hart and Keliher ox-drawn freight wagons, hauling heavy mining equipment from the East before the building of the railroad, pause at Rapid City. By the 1880's companies able to afford deep-shaft mining were replacing individual gold-seekers like the one on the preceding page.

An early mining town, above, sits in a pocket in the Black Hills.

Primitive stores built of logs and rough boards supplied "grub" and basic necessities, usually at inflated prices, to the inhabitants of the isolated mining settlements.

At right, a flume, carrying water by gravity, for hydraulic mining, crosses a ravine.

In front of a trim home in the Hills, a caulked log cabin complete with window curtain and picket fence, miners pose proudly for a picture to send back home.

The huge Open Cut at Lead, opposite, resulted from the cave-in of a mine. The gash expanded yearly, eating away at the gold center's streets and buildings.

In inset, tents and false fronts line the main street of a settlement in the pine-covered hills.

OPPOSITE: Headquarters of a tin mine. Until it was discovered near Hill City in 1883, all tin in the U.S. was imported.

LEFT: Dressed in Sunday best and displaying his tools and other possessions, a miner named Conrad Liston poses before his cabin (and a deer trophy) for a photograph, possibly by M. A. Fuller, to send to relatives.

BELOW: Freight wagons on their way to Rockerville (named for the number of rockers used by the miners) and Keystone, south of Rapid City.

ABOVE: Employees of the Tenderfoot Tin Mine near Custer.

LEFT: In 1876, after news of a rich gold strike in Deadwood Gulch, 25,000 people poured into the narrow valley and built the boisterous town of Deadwood. The most famous mining center in the Black Hills, it survived a disastrous fire in 1879 and a flood in 1883.

LEFT: Cars drawn on rails by horses, often directed by young boys (overleaf), brought ore out of the deep mines.

BELOW, LEFT AND RIGHT: The photographer pictured hillside mine buildings in summer and winter.

29

Typical mine installations in the Hills housed ore mills and hoisting machinery over the deep shafts.

ABOVE: The structures of the Lundberg, Dorr, and Wilson Mill at Terry on the slope of Bald Mountain. When this picture was taken, about 1910, the Burlington Railroad had reached Terry which had a population of 1,000.

RIGHT: The hoisting machinery over the mine shaft.

OVERLEAF: Air compressor equipment at one of the mines.

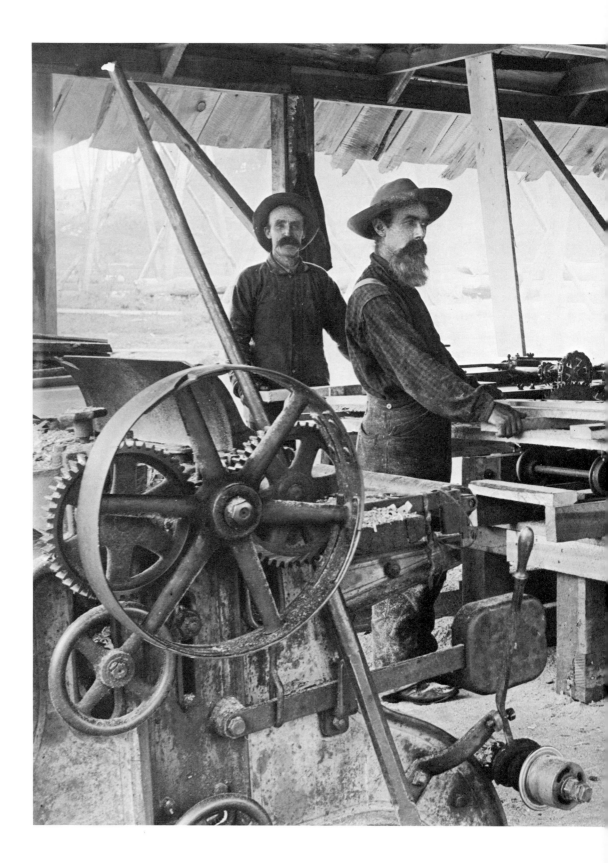

Lumber

From the start of the gold rush, the great pine stands of the Black Hills provided lumber for the mines and new settlements. The arduous whipsawing of logs was quickly replaced by the arrival of portable, and then permanent, steam sawmills and plane mills like the one above.

Scores of small business establishments that sprang up throughout the Hills were built with the rough boards of the early sawmills. This is the shop of a blacksmith and wagon mender.

The sawmills, using oxen and mules to haul logs from the woods (above), supplied miners with lumber for flumes, sluice boxes, and stulls and caps that supported the roofs of deep mines.

At right is a large operation of later days, the W. H. Holstein sawmill and lumber yard in Stage Barn Canyon between Rapid City and Sturgis.

As the towns grew, the sawmills dotting the Black Hills could scarcely keep up with the demand for manufactured lumber. Three mills in Deadwood produced 32,000 board feet a day. Around Custer eventually there were twenty mills employing some 250 men.

In time, logging became big business. The railroad replaced oxen and mules, and small mills like the one at upper left were hard put to compete with large, well-financed lumber companies which even exported timber to distant markets.

The Warren-Lamb Lumber Company loads newly harvested logs on railroad flatcars, above.

The Guardians

For a long time the Black Hills was an island in territory that still belonged to the Indians, many of whom were angry over the way the Hills had been taken from them. Though the tribes were now pacified and forced to stay near agencies, cavalry units like the one above were based near the mines and settlements to keep an eye on the Indians and prevent trouble.

Reconstituted after its 1876 defeat at the Little Bighorn, the
Seventh Cavalry (some of whose troopers are seen below)
was one of the units based near Sturgis at Fort Meade,
shown here with Bear Butte in the background.

The Indians at Pine Ridge and other Sioux reservations in Dakota Territory were favorite subjects for the Rapid City photographers who traveled to their camps to take their pictures.

BELOW: Indians at a dance have paused to gather around the drummers for this group photograph.

The face of the Indian-fighting army: Cavalry troopers in wide-brimmed hats, looking like subjects of a Frederic Remington painting, were photographed on the sage plains along the eastern side of the Black Hills.

Roaming the nearby Dakota reservations, the photographers continued to picture the defeated and dejected Sioux. It was a harsh period for the Indians: Government agents, many of them corrupt, were trying to make them give up their old ways of life and also sign away large areas of their land.

ABOVE: Several Indians are shown with government agents, who attempted with little success to turn them into farmers.

RIGHT: A proud Sioux family, already on the road to acculturation, was photographed by W. J. Collins in his Rapid City studio.

Roads and Railroads

The Black Hills provided its early inhabitants with special problems of transportation and communication. Railroads at first could not cross Indian lands to reach the booming region. Within the Hills, rugged terrain and rain and snow storms often isolated camps and settlements. But roads for stages and freight wagons were stubbornly pushed through the mountains, and in the 1880's agreements with the Indians finally permitted railroad surveyors like the group above to lay out routes that would connect the mining centers with the main lines in Nebraska.

Deep in the Hills, construction gangs graded routes that aided the movement of supplies to each new location where a strike had been made.

In inset is a typical pioneering camp of placer miners, using sluices and living in tents. Strips of venison dry above the keg top, and their covered wagon sits in the background.

The presence of the surveyors and construction gangs were exciting to the Black Hills residents, for they symbolized practical improvements and progress. To the photographers who journeyed through the Hills to record their activities, they represented history in the making.

A surveyor and his family at home in the Hills.

Construction crews in the field and a view of a completed rail line arching through Dark Canyon to connect Rapid City with the mining centers of Pactola, Silver City, Rochford, and Castleton in the central Hills.

By the start of the 1890's, both the North Western and the Burlington Railroads had completed branch lines from Nebraska that wound through the Hills and spelled the beginning of the end for the freight wagon and stagecoach companies.

TOP LEFT: A view of the tracks through the intensively mined Nevada Gulch near Terry.

LEFT: Locomotives chug into Deadwood after a winter storm.

ABOVE: Rails are laid on a horseshoe curve between Hill City and Custer.

This long trestle bridge, shown being completed in 1890, carried the Burlington tracks over Sheep Canyon between Edgemont and Pringle in the southern Hills.

FAREWELL TO THE BUFFALO

The Cowmen

To break the last resistance of the plains Indians, the army encouraged the slaughter of the buffalo on which the tribes depended for their existence. By the end of the 1870's, meat and robe hunters had almost wiped out the huge herds. In their place, feeding on the vast, empty ranges of rich grama and buffalo grass, came cattle, driven up the long trails from Texas. Some of the best rangeland was in western Dakota, and soon, thriving cattle ranches and tough, hard-riding cowboys (seen here with their horses) were a fixture on the grazing lands that bordered the Black Hills.

The busiest time on the ranches was during the fall round-ups, left. Note the herds being held in the distance as animals are sorted out. The high-spirited cowboys were colorful subjects for the Black Hills photographers, often striking playful and humorous poses for the camera.

The period 1880-1900 saw the cowboy of the West become a genuine American folk hero, and much of the mystique about him was created on the ranches and in the towns of the Black Hills. Among those spreading his fame was a woman who had entered the Hills with the first gold-seeking party in 1874, Annie D. Tallent. In an 1899 history of the area, she wrote: "I must confess here to something of an admiration for cowboys . . . they have been known to fire random shots as they dashed along the streets of certain towns of the Hills . . . and to ride their bronchos, roughshod, through the doors and up to the bars of saloons, and such playful pranks, but, after all, they are, in many respects, very manly fellows. They are perfect types of muscular development, endure hardships that would kill an ordinary mortal, are dead shots and the most expert horsemen in the world. . . . The average cowboy is honest, kindhearted, generous to a fault, and, in short, is not half so bad as he is painted."

The first cowboys in the Black Hills had learned their trade in the Southwest and on the trail drives north, and they influenced range life in the Hills. Opposite are scenes around the celebrated chuckwagon that followed the cowboys with their meals and bedrolls. Depending on the cook's skills, supplies, and inclination, a meal might include fried meat, sourdough biscuits, white gravy, beans, canned corn, and dried fruit. Coffee, kept hot in a big pot by the fire, was always the staple. The top scene seems to be an evening meal, because bedrolls are in evidence.

These scenes of ranchers, with their families and hands, were taken at roundup time. Most of the biggest spreads lay north and south of the Hills, in the grassland valleys of the Belle Fourche River and the South Fork of the Cheyenne.

One of the Black Hills' best-known ranchers, Corbin Morse, was photographed at the fireplace in his ranch home by W. J. Collins. Morse, a bachelor and a man respected as a good judge of beef cattle, owned a large ranch east of Rapid City. He suffered a severe reverse in 1905 when he lost most of his herd in a winter storm.

Another well-known cattleman, Frank Hart, owned a ranch at Scenic near the Badlands east of the Hills. Hart was also a top bronc buster. He was photographed against a wooded backdrop in Collins' Rapid City studio, showing off what may have been a saddle won in a bronc-busting contest early in this century.

Cattle branding on a Stock Ranch

Cowboys at play in town, opposite, and at serious work,
below, branding cattle on a stock ranch.

Corbin Morse and friends out for a ride near the home and
headquarters buildings of his prosperous 6L Ranch.

Settlers

Western Dakota Territory was one of the last parts of the nation opened to homesteaders. After 1877, when the government finally forced the Sioux to cede the
Black Hills, the region could be legally settled. Farmers and their families, like
those above, photographed on their arrival at Hermosa, traveled to the Hills to
claim free land and make a new start in life.

Most of the first homesteaders, with their meager possessions,
traveled to the new land of promise in covered wagons.
This family was photographed by Collins soon after it
reached the Hills.

As the photographers visited the newcomers, who paid them with food or small articles, rather than cash, for pictures which the settlers could send to relatives back home, they recorded the pioneering life. For a while, some homesteaders lived in tents while they put in a crop. Others raised rough log cabins. In time, with hard work, sacrifice, and luck, families made it, like the group opposite. Emigrants from Scandinavia, they pose proudly in their best clothes (brought from the old country) to show off their neat new American homestead.

Education was not forgotten, and small,
rough-timbered schools soon dotted the
Black Hills. These pictures of frontier
teachers and children were made by Fuller
and Collins in the 1880's and 1890's.

ABOVE: A farm family in the Hills. Their tarpaper-covered home is battened down with boards.

OPPOSITE: Water for the family tub and other uses was hauled from nearby creeks or springs.

OVERLEAF: Settlers display their saddle horses and other possessions, even a broom, in pictures of their two-story homes.

Growing prosperity: Outbuildings, stockyards, farm equipment, and wagons. In taking large view pictures, the photographers carefully positioned people and their possessions, not only for composition, but so that everything might be noticed.

M. A. Fuller's darkroom wagon is seen above, in the background of the hay yard on the farm which he or his assistant, William F. Hall, had come to photograph.

At right, horses, oxen, men, and equipment at work on a large farm in the Hills.

After the railroads reached the Black Hills, they brought many industrious emigrant settlers, including Finns, other Scandinavians, and Germans. The type of haystack seen above reflects a European origin. In the carefully arranged picture, the man at center is on a mower, the woman at right on a hay rake.

The dream come true: A two-story rural home with bay
windows and a birdcage hanging over a shaded porch. 111

The Gentry

Within the towns of the Black Hills, as people in the trades and businesses made money, homes became grander. Manufactured goods, imported from the cities of the Midwest and the East, made life more gracious. Though it was hard sometimes to remember that this was still frontier, the children raised in these homes would one day look back on their parents as pioneers who had established civilization where there had been none before.

These pictures of townspeople and typical homes in Rapid City were taken by W. J. Collins in the 1890's and early 1900's. Most houses were white clapboard and had front stoops or porches with ornate posts and scrollwork. The croquet players at lower right are outside the home of a Rapid City doctor, Dan Whitfield.

ABOVE: A large town house shows signs of affluence—lightning rods, painted trim, a hobbyhorse, bird cages, and a hammock.

LEFT: A more modest home with a covered entry and a bay window.

RIGHT: A young woman uses a baby buggy and a bucket for clothespins to hang out the wash.

Collins also pictured townspeople in their buggies visiting friends in the country and viewing the scenic splendors of the Black Hills. The handsome gabled home at Custer, above, belonged to Joseph Pilcher.

The age of the horse.

LEFT: A Sunday ride in the Hills.

BELOW: Showing off stock.

Two elegant Rapid City homes. The tall brick structure, left, with bay windows on two stories, was built by a Captain Davis on West Boulevard. In the 1960's it became a home for retarded children. The landscaped residence, above, between Sixth and Seventh on Quincy Street, belonged to Miron Wilsie. Looming beyond it is the spire of the Congregational church.

A Collins' photograph of the sitting room in a late-nineteenth-century home in Rapid City. Note the imported tiled fireplace and the local South Dakota stuffed grouse above the mantel.

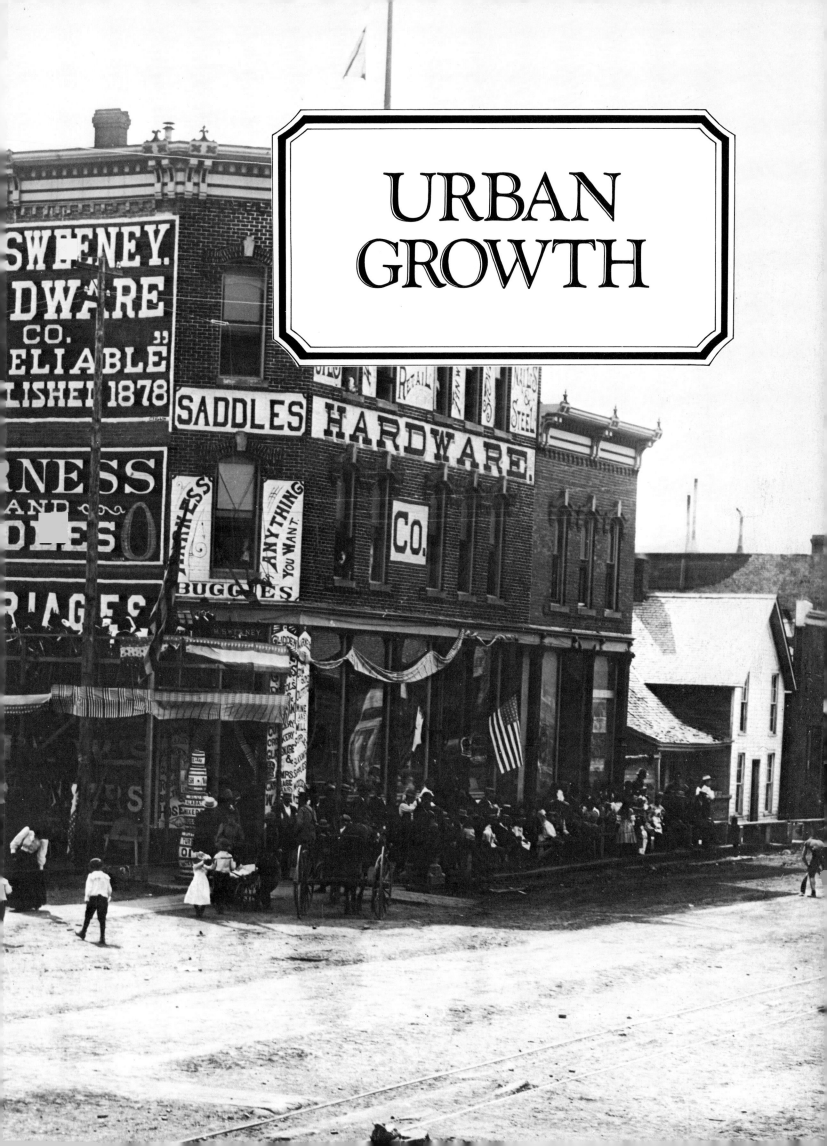

URBAN GROWTH

Cities in the Hills

The oldest town in the Black Hills, Custer, was staked out in 1875 by miners on French Creek, near the site of the first gold discovery. Originally called Stonewall, for Confederate General "Stonewall" Jackson, it was renamed to honor Custer after his death. The view above was made soon after 1881, when the town, with a population of 400, got its first brick building, the two-story county courthouse, seen at center. On the preceding page is a Collins photograph of the Rapid City business building of Thomas Sweeney, who arrived in the Hills penniless in 1877 and began his rise by borrowing a razor and setting himself up as a barber.

ABOVE: Residents of a Black Hills town pose on the board sidewalk.

LEFT: Hill City, the second settlement in the Hills, had ups and downs as a gold center, then boomed again in 1883 (six years before this picture was taken) with the discovery of tin nearby.

The second major gold strike in the Hills led to the founding of Deadwood in a narrow gulch.

LEFT: The stagecoach in a picture probably made by one of Collins' predecessors is seen on the city's single, long main street which usually teemed with traffic.

BELOW: Farmland, loans, agricultural equipment, and legal advice could all be procured in this typical Black Hills business office.

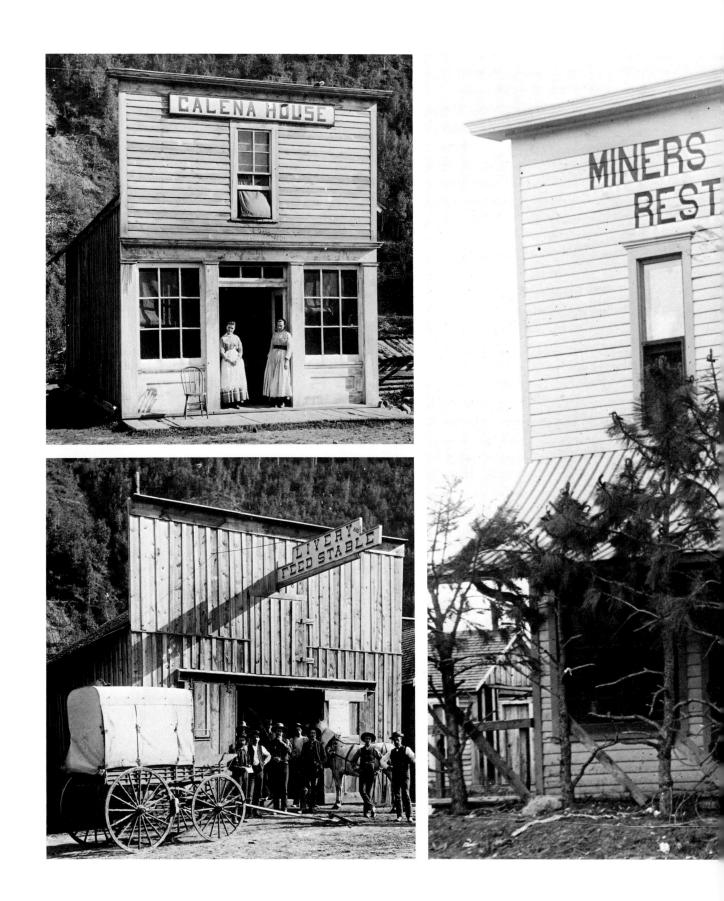

THE EXCHANGE
AURANT.

The neat and homey Galena House, upper left, catered to
residents of the Galena silver-mining district near Deadwood;
the livery stable was in Keystone, an important mining
town near Mount Rushmore; and the large restaurant, above,
was at Hermosa on the eastern fringe of the Hills.

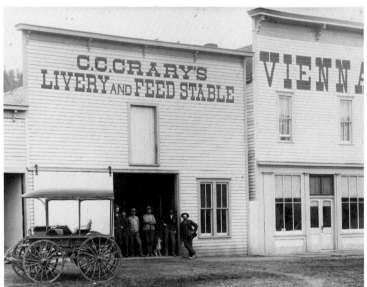

Collins made these photographs of businesses in Custer around the turn of the century. The Vienna Hotel, next to C. C. Crary's livery stable, above, burned down soon after the picture was taken.

At right, proprietor J. M. Flowers, his wife and child, the cook, and town residents stand outside the Star Restaurant where Flowers served meals ("Lunch at all hours") for thirty-five cents.

D. W. Webster's general store, left, was in Hill City. In this carefully arranged photograph by Collins of four ladies in a spring wagon and a sport with his high-wheeled bike, Mr. Webster can be seen on the boardwalk on the other side of the horses.

Above is another Hill City store that purveyed almost everything—for the dead as well as the living.

TOP LEFT: The Grand Army of the Republic (Union veterans of the Civil War) and the Masons, side by side in Hill City.

LEFT: A brass band, assembled for a holiday occasion.

ABOVE: A street scene in an unidentified town. Note: Where were the women?

A close-up view of Custer's $12,000 county courthouse, seen from afar on pages 128-129.

At right is a late-nineteenth-century Collins photograph of residents of Hermosa outside a building housing a general store and a doctor's office.

Rapid City

Frontier-type false fronts still mingle with two- and three-story stone and brick commercial buildings in this 1907 Collins photograph of a women's riding group assembled for a parade on Main Street in Rapid City, the Black Hills' principal transportation and business center.

Founded on the eastern edge of the Hills in February, 1876, Rapid City was a supply base for all the mining towns, whose residents called it the "Hay Camp."

TOP LEFT: A tree on Hangman's Hill, overlooking the town, from which three men were hanged in 1887, "by unknown parties," for horse stealing.

TOP RIGHT AND LOWER LEFT: Stagecoaches and mule-drawn freight wagons linked Rapid City with the Hill towns and the outside world.

ABOVE: An early view of the city.

FAR LEFT: Collins' daughter is in the foreground of this overall view of the plains terrain on which Rapid City grew.

LEFT: This handsome commercial building was one of several erected by Robert Florman who settled in Rapid City about 1885 after a long career in mining.

BELOW: Bricks for Rapid City buildings were produced at the Marshall brickyard on Deadwood Avenue north of the town.

The huge tree above, planted in 1878, was owned by P. B. McCarthy, proprietor of Rapid City's oldest hotel, the International. It shaded the stand of waiting stages of the Northwestern Stage & Transportation Line that ran between Deadwood and Pierre on the Missouri River, by way of Rapid City.

At right, children and their teachers pose outside the city's public school building, erected in 1882. Earlier, classes were taught in rented buildings.

The Bishop Ware School, top left, was built in the 1880's on the outskirts of Rapid City as an Episcopal Mission home for Sioux Indian children. In 1900, during an outbreak of smallpox, it was used as a pest house for the ill. Below it is the high school, with its bell tower and chimneys, built in 1885 on high ground overlooking the city. Above are a grade school teacher and her pupils, posed with appropriately serious expressions for their school picture.

The building at top left housed the hose and equipment of a Rapid City fire-fighting company. The scene above was found in Collins' collection. It seems to show a salesman demonstrating the tightening of a buggy belt.

The City Hall in Rapid City, opposite, built in 1903, on Sixth Street between St. Joe and Kansas City Streets, is still in existence. But the sixty-five-foot-high firebell tower, erected behind it (left), disappeared in 1915.

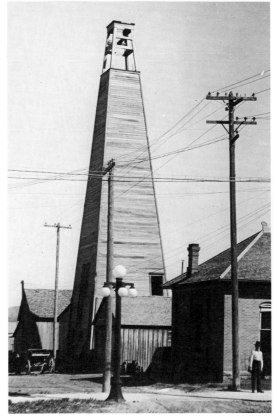

155

Conquered, demoralized, and no longer a threat to the whites, the impoverished Indians on the nearby reservations were regarded patronizingly as picturesque and colorful. For small rewards, they occasionally came to Rapid City to participate and dance in civic functions. At one such affair, in 1903, they joined some white residents of the town for a group picture by Collins around a Major Fred Bennett (above), a noted stilt walker.

The Collins photograph at right, taken in 1893, shows Sioux doing war dances at the intersection of Main and Sixth Streets in Rapid City—an annual event during which the spectators pitched coins to the Indians. Eventually, some of the Rapid City women complained of the Indians' nudity, and thereafter the dancers performed in long underwear.

LEFT: In 1907 the Milwaukee Railroad finally reached Rapid City from the East, and war-bonneted Sioux obligingly lent their presence to a celebration of the occasion.

TOP: The onion-domed Buell Building at St. Joe and Seventh Streets, housing the U.S. Land Office, is still a prominent structure in downtown Rapid City. The wide streets were planned to allow oxtrains to turn around in them.

ABOVE: The Eureka Auditorium, built originally in the 1890's as a skating rink, and then converted into a horse barn, was refurbished by a Doctor Derthick in 1907 for dances, roller skating, minstrel shows, and theatricals. It later became a movie theater and burned down in 1927.

Every town in the Hills had a volunteer fire department, and the annual Firemen's Tournaments, with hook-and-ladder races, ladder-climbing contests, and other competitions, were big events. Shown here, at the 1896 tournament in Rapid City, are running teams who pulled their hose carts in races through the streets. The colorful tourneys ended when the towns adopted fire trucks.

ABOVE: Twentieth-century progress in Rapid City—laying out a concrete sidewalk.

LEFT: The maturing city—in the center is a large, new Catholic church; the smaller, old one is to its right. Far on the horizon is the Bishop Ware Mission School for Indians.

At left is the Methodist Episcopal church, one of the first organized in Rapid City.

Above is the Methodist Deaconess Hospital, previously the private home of the builder of a railroad line up Rapid Canyon.

In 1880, public-spirited citizens organized a Library Association in Rapid City to "provide amusement for winter nights." After first leasing a room, the Association constructed a Library Hall (above) in 1881, on land at Kansas City and Sixth Streets donated by John R. Brennan, one of the founders of the city. In ensuing years, the building was also used for lectures, concerts, dances, and political debates.

Soon after the first gold strikes, enterprising journalists arrived in the Black Hills with presses, type, paper, and ink in their wagons to start newspapers for the miners. Filled with information about the different camps, discussions of public questions (such as Indian problems and free silver) which affected the region, and advertisements that brought together newly arrived buyers and sellers, the papers were avidly read and helped the expanding business life of the Hills. Some of the papers existed for a long time; others flourished briefly and then disappeared. The *Weekly Democrat* (opposite) was published in Rapid City from 1887 to 1896. Collins' waggish photograph, probably of the paper's first publisher, G. W. Barrows, peering through a blowup of the news and advertisements on the front page, may have been taken to mount as a humorous poster for a dinner or other local event.

The Commercial Life

A sampling of goods and services provided by Rapid City
entrepreneurs, as recorded in Collins' photographs.

The Pennington County Bank in Rapid City, opposite, was opened for business in 1888 and was the largest state bank in South Dakota, with capital stock of $50,000.

The wintry scene of the foundry and windmill beyond it, above, is also in Rapid City.

The lumber and construction supply business at left was at Sixth and St. Joe Streets in Rapid City. The automobiles and street lights show that the photograph is of relatively late vintage.

The big smelter, above, with a 140-foot-high smokestack, marked the coming of heavy industry to Rapid City. It was built in 1902 to extract gold from types of ore that could not be processed in stamp mills.

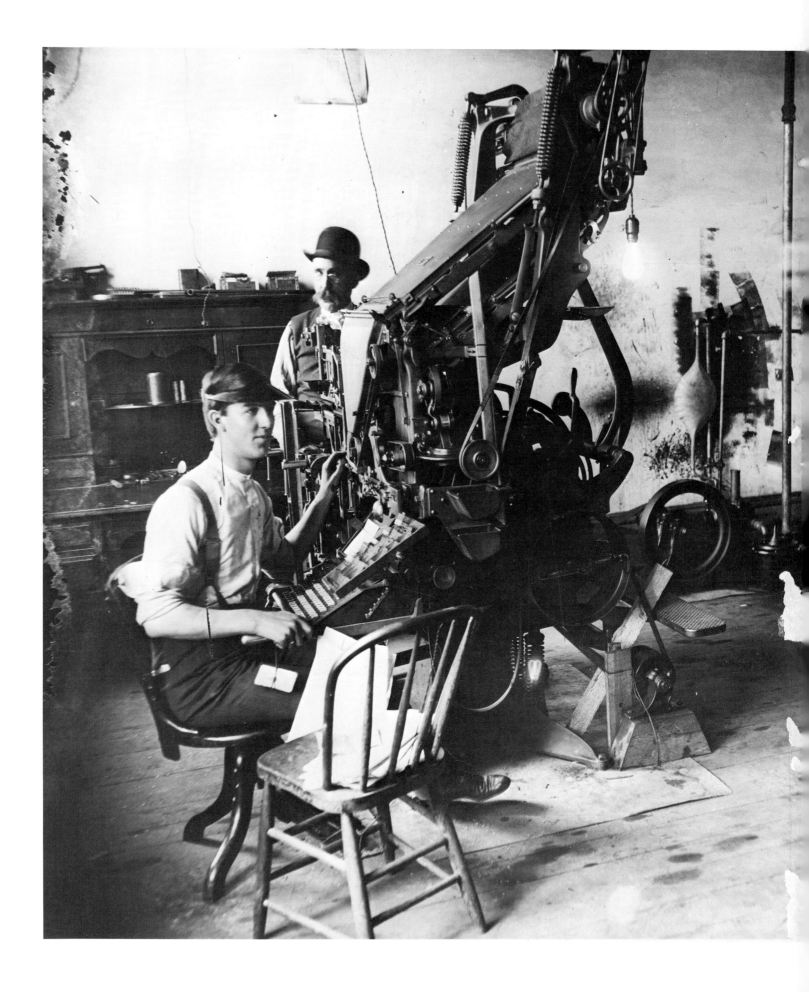

Rapid City's first newspaper, the *Journal*, founded in 1878, is still published. On May 10, 1905, it got its first linotype machine, powered by a gas-fueled, one-and-a-half-horsepower engine, and Collins photographed it (left), showing the proud operator, Frank Benham, and the newspaper's publisher, Joseph B. Gossage (in derby).

Below are businessmen on a hardware store's horse-drawn float during the 1907 celebration of the coming of the Milwaukee Railroad to Rapid City. Duhamel's, founded by Peter Duhamel who is on the float and who once ran 10,000 head of cattle on the Bad River range, is still one of Rapid City's principal stores.

The Milwaukee Railroad provided the first through-car railroad service between Rapid City and Chicago, and the arrival of the first train from Chicago on July 20, 1907, was hailed by a parade and a "Jubilee" celebration. This scene of riders and a meat market's bunting-draped entry before the start of the parade was taken on Main Street, looking west from Sixth Street.

ABOVE: Photographer Collins' daughter, Beulah, was among the women on this carriage, a millinery shop's entry in the 1907 Railroad Jubilee parade.

RIGHT: The interior of a well-stocked men's clothing store. The flowers suggest that the picture was taken on a special occasion, perhaps the day of the store's opening.

OVERLEAF: A Rapid City jewelry store, festooned for the peak sales days before Christmas. The costly appointments and wares are signs that the frontier period was already far in the past.

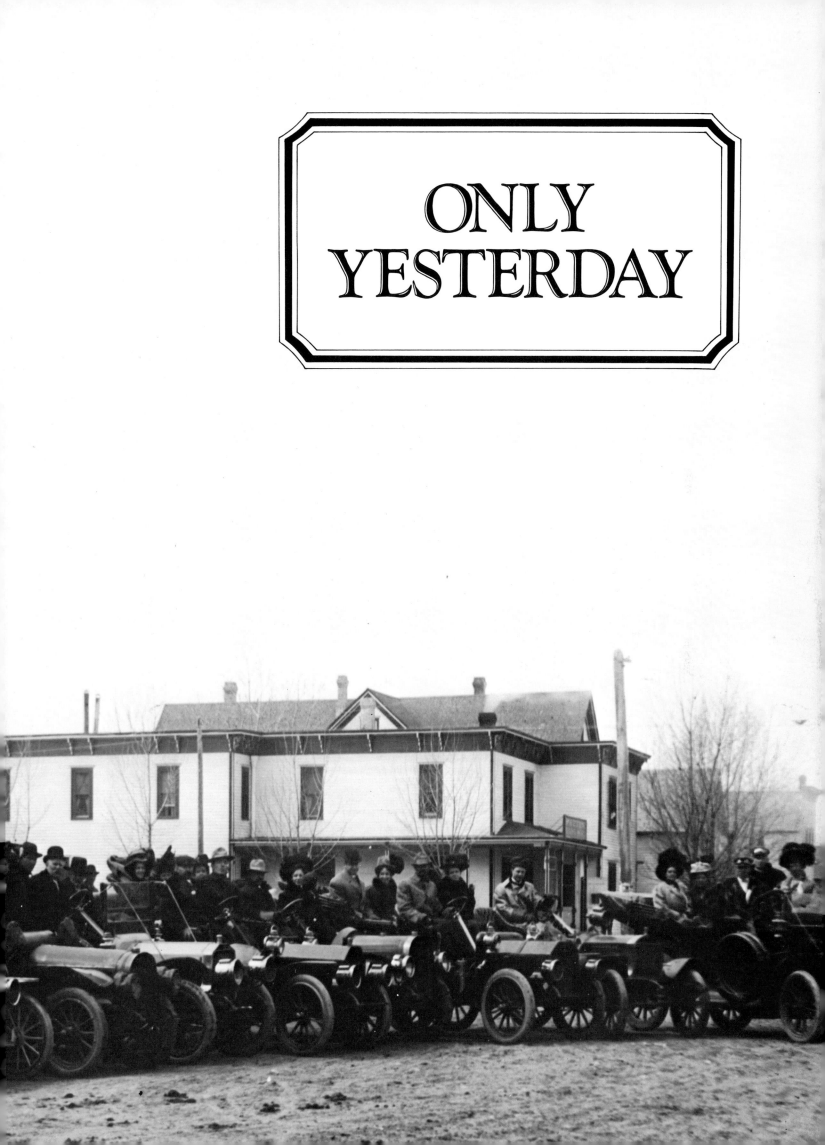

ONLY
YESTERDAY

Its beauty, natural wonders, and cool summer climate destined the Black Hills to become one of the nation's most popular resort areas. At first, its charms and splendors were almost the private preserve of those who lived in the region. But eventually their fame spread, and visitors came in increasing numbers, putting up at the local hotels and touring the Hills in carriages. One of the first attractions to gain national attention were thermal waters, discovered in the late 1870's along Fall River in the southern Hills. The town of Hot Springs was founded, and the

The First Resorts

waters—advertised as beneficial for whatever ailed a person—lured those with
rheumatism and other physical complaints from all over the country to the spa's
baths and splendid resort hotels like the Minnekahta (above). The influx of out-
siders gave birth to a tourist industry centered at Rapid City, and with the coming
of the automobile, companies did a thriving business transporting sightseers to
the colorful towns and scenic attractions of the Hills in open, gas-driven touring
cars (preceding page).

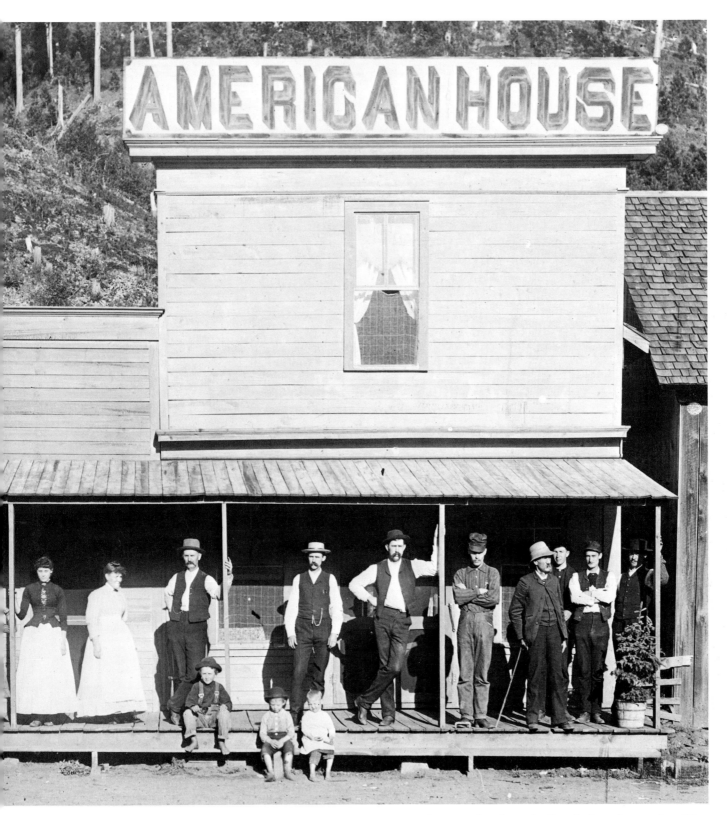

Two early rustic hotels in the days before the tourists. The residents were principally mining people and their families, itinerants, and traveling salesmen.

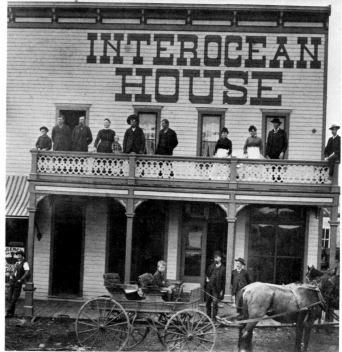

As the trade increased and more was demanded in the way of comfort and service, the hotels became larger and more attractive. The Scollard, with a hammock on its second-story shaded porch at Sturgis, was owned by John Scollard who, during the 1876 mining rush, had built a hotel at Deadwood. The elegant brick Kleemann House was at Custer, and the Battle River House was at Hermosa. The Interocean House, location unknown, seems to have been named after a popular hostelry in Cheyenne.

The International at Fifth and Main Streets was Rapid City's oldest hotel. Built in 1878, it was taken over and operated by P. B. McCarthy. Stockmen made it their headquarters when they gathered in Rapid City for business meetings and to hire hands for their ranches (top).

The lower picture shows a horse-drawn street car passing the hotel. The tracks were laid for about a mile along the center of Main Street by the Rapid City Street Railway Company in 1886 at a cost of $7,000.

The kerosene-lit dining room of McCarthy's International Hotel, above, was cheerful, if not elegant, and the fare, it is safe to assume, was hearty. A suggestion of what may have been on the menu is seen at the right, in one of Collins' staged photographs. Wild game, including ducks, geese, and venison, was abundant in the Black Hills.

The warm, healing waters of Fall River and its adjoining springs and pools were known to the Sioux Indians before they were ousted from the Black Hills. When the whites came upon the phenomenon, they established the town of Hot Springs, which soon boomed as an "American Carlsbad." By the 1890's, the hotels, baths, and plunges were a mecca for visitors from all over the country who were afflicted with maladies that ranged from dyspepsia to deformed limbs. Others simply went there to enjoy a pleasant vacation and drink the water to feel even better than they did (opposite page).

At left and below is the turreted, sandstone Gillespie Hotel, a popular center at the Springs, built by Fred Gillespie in 1890 at a cost of $25,000.

The passage of time is vividly revealed in these photographs of Rapid City's three-story, brick Harney Hotel. Operated in the nineteenth century by John R. Brennan, one of the city's founders, who built Rapid City's first hotel—a twelve-by fourteen-foot log structure—in 1876, the Harney had fifty rooms and was for many decades, the principal hotel in the city. Both pictures were taken by Collins from the same spot on the corner of Sixth and Main Streets. The one at left, showing a mule-drawn stage crossing a street ditch that carried away rain water, must have been made soon after the hotel opened for business in 1886. In the twentieth-century view above, automobiles, street lamps, and a modern loan and trust company have been added to the scene of the "New Harney," but the ditches and crosswalks are still there. At left is one of the early automobiles in Rapid City.

LEFT: A vignette at Hot Springs. At rear are the side porches of the Minnekahta Hotel.

ABOVE: The stagecoaches and freight wagons are gone. Another Collins photograph of an early automobile, symbol of a new era in the Black Hills and in America.

By 1900, the miners, ranchers, settlers, and merchants of the first generation in the Black Hills were already regarded as pioneers, whose hardships, struggles, and triumphs had brought civilization to this part of the western frontier. Collins had photographed many of them at home and at work, at outings and picnics in the Hills (above), and in his Rapid City studio near the Harney Hotel. He

O Pioneers

continued to photograph their children and their children's children until his retirement in 1933. On the following pages are some of his pictures of these generations of builders of the Black Hills, many of them forgotten, some perhaps still alive or known to those still living. They were pioneers all.

Joe Hinkle was a bullwhacker who drove ox teams in the pre-railroad days of the freight wagons. He settled down near Piedmont at the eastern foot of the Hills, and, for many years, friends remembered the strawberries that he grew there.

Charles H. Howard got into a scrape in Sioux Falls, South
Dakota, where he had been county treasurer. He moved to
the Black Hills, successfully took up ranching northeast of
Rapid City, and became one of the first presidents of the
South Dakota Stockgrowers Association.

TOP LEFT: Descendants of the first residents of the Black Hills: Young Sioux men and women being turned into whites—uniforms, haircuts, disciplined posture, and all —at the U.S. Government's Indian School at Rapid City early in the twentieth century.

ABOVE AND LEFT: Unidentified residents of the Hills, in Collins' studio and at an outing.

This personable young lady in a Lillian Russell hat was named, according to Collins, May Moon.

The dapper Joseph Poznansky ran a dry goods store in
Sturgis. His father, Felix, was a pioneer Jewish merchant
and civic leader in Rapid City, who helped plan the city's
first waterworks and served on the city council.

One would give a lot, today, to know something about the two poised and festively garbed young ladies opposite. Collins left no clue.

The family above, photographed in Collins' studio, seems somewhat fresh from the old country, and perhaps had this picture taken to send back to relatives.

ABOVE: Was this a trouping thespian, done up as Othello for a one-night stand in Rapid City—or perhaps a local citizen in an amateur theatrical at Derthick's auditorium?

RIGHT: An imaginative Collins studio portrait—"Woman at Gate."

CLOCKWISE FROM UPPER LEFT: Dr. P. J. Waldron of Rapid City; James "Scotty" Philip, who, when the buffalo were almost exterminated, built up a herd of his own and saved them from extinction (his animals began the Custer State Park herd); unknown; John P. McElroy, star Rapid City athlete and fire department chief.

Taking water at a spring. Collins left no record of who these men were, where they were, or what (if anything, other than getting some water) was going on.

Another mystery. These dandies are obviously dressed up for something and are having fun. But why the rope?

These are Ute Indians who had fled into Wyoming from white oppressors in Utah, in 1906. The government herded them to Fort Meade and put them to work on the railroad lines and repairing fences in Rapid City, where Collins photographed them in his studio. The man proudly holding the eagle feathers is a spiritual leader of his people. The Indians were later returned peaceably to Utah by the cavalry.

The band at left was organized and financed by F. N. Emrick, a Rapid City dentist and Exalted Ruler of the Elks, who also became mayor of the city.

The South Dakota militia unit below was photographed in Rapid City in 1898 as it was about to depart for the Spanish-American War.

Another Ute Indian exile in Rapid City, 1907.

A bridal picture—one of Collins' specialties.

The years creep on, and customs change. A mixed-sex card game and a fashion "still" in the 1920's era of bobbed hair and flaming youth.

Collins missed little in Rapid City—
prominent citizens in an early touring car,
above, and the town's 1904 baseball team,
at right.

OVERLEAF: In his last years as a photographer, Collins took artistic poses in his
studio, sometimes using his daughter, Mrs.
Beulah Crockett, as his model. If he had
gone on photographing, he undoubtedly
would have recorded the Black Hills of the
Depression, of the stone faces at Mount
Rushmore, of World War II, and of the
great post-war tourist boom. But he finally
put away his camera and died in 1938.